Apples, Bubbles, and Crystals

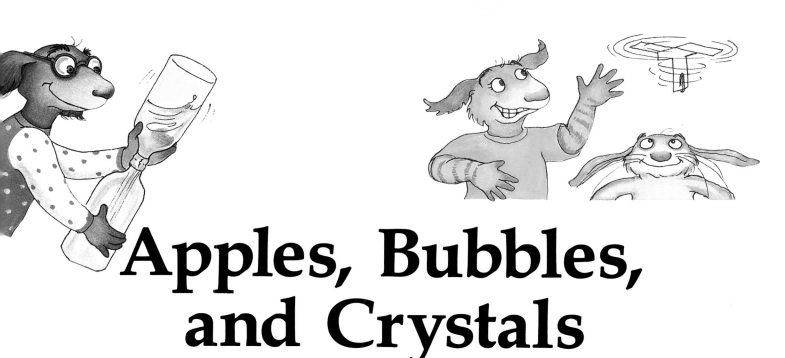

Apples, Bubbles, and Crystals

Your Science ABCs

Andrea T. Bennett
James H. Kessler
Illustrated by Melody Sarecky

LEARNING
TRIANGLE
PRESS

©1996 by The American Chemical Society.
Published by The McGraw-Hill Companies, Inc.

pbk 4 5 6 7 8 9 10 KKP/KKP 9 0 0 9 8 7

Library of Congress Cataloging-in-Publication Data

Bennett, Andrea T.
    Apples, bubbles, & crystals : your science ABCs / by Andrea T. Bennett
and James Kessler ; illustrated by Melody Sarecky.
        p.   cm.
    Includes index.
    Summary: Each letter of the alphabet is represented by a poem and
some type of science experiment or activity. Explanations of the
scientific principles involved are given at the end of the book.
    ISBN 0-07-005827-X (P)
    1. Science—Experiments—Juvenile literature. 2. Science—Study
and teaching (Elementary)—Activity programs. [1. Science-
-Experiments. 2. Experiments. 3. Alphabet.] I. Kessler, James H.
II. Sarecky, Melody, ill.
Q164.B46   1996
507.8—dc   95-50309
                                                                    CIP
                                                                     AC

McGraw-Hill books are available at special quantity discounts to use as premiums and sales promotions, or for use in corporate training programs. For more information, please write to the Director of Special Sales, McGraw-Hill, 11 West 19th Street, New York, NY 10011. Or contact your local bookstore.

Acquisitions editor: Judith Terrill-Breuer, Editor-in-Chief
Editorial team: Robert E. Ostrander, Executive Editor
                        John C. Baker, Book Editor
Production team: Katherine G. Brown, Director
                        Linda M. Cramer, Proofreading
Design team: Jaclyn J. Boone, Designer
                        Katherine Lukaszewicz, Associate Designer   005827X

Dear Fellow Parents and Teachers:

For all of us, the years of early childhood are years of challenge and opportunity. It is a challenge to find the time and energy to answer the many questions children ask—questions of how? where? why? when? and what? However, we have a unique opportunity, too, because the child asking questions is a child looking around with wonder and curiosity, a child seeking to understand the amazing world in which we live, eager to explore the unknown. The young child is a natural scientist!

Through interactions with children, we can help them grow into adults who retain that wonder and curiosity, or we can extinguish the spark forever. A child who is not encouraged to explore eventually might lose all interest in exploration.

The science activities in this book are designed for children who ask questions and the adults who care about keeping that spark burning. They are designed for you to do together so that supervision (always necessary for science experiments with young children) and sharing become one. We hope you and the child in your life have an absolutely wonderful time reading our poems and doing the activities. This is what science is all about—looking at the world with the eyes of a child, making some sense of the mystery, and looking again with deeper wonder.

Sylvia A. Ware

Sylvia Ware, Director
Education Division
American Chemical Society

Aa is for apple.

Meet Archie of the orchard,
An apple kind of guy.
He picks a batch, then cooks them
For apple sauce and pie.

When Archie cuts up apples,
The slices all turn brown.
They don't look very yummy,
Which makes his buddies frown.

But Archie is a good cook
Who knows a special way
To stop the color changing
At any time of day!

APPLES WITH APPEAL

What You'll Need:
- paper towels
- 1 sheet of paper
- 3 apple pieces
- lemon juice
- water

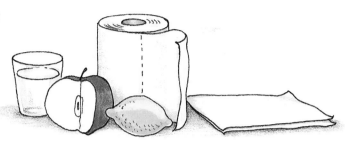

Bb is for bubble.

Benny bought a bubble loop
For bubbles big and small.
He blew so many bubbles,
He couldn't count them all.

Along came Benny's brother,
Who's always on the run.
He spilled the bubble liquid,
Which ruined Benny's fun.

Benny did not get upset.
He knew what he could do.
He made more bubble liquid.
It's easy—you can, too!

BUBBLES WITHOUT TROUBLES

What You'll Need:
- 1/2 cup dishwashing liquid
- 2 cups water
- 1 teaspoon sugar
- shallow baking pan
- plastic strawberry basket
- plastic straw
- pipe cleaners
- measuring cup and spoons

1. Add detergent and sugar to water. Stir. Pour solution in a shallow pan.

solution goes here

2. Dip straw tip in bubble liquid. Blow bubbles!

Be careful not to suck up the soap solution through the straw!

3. Twist pipe cleaners into bubble makers.

twist into shape

4. Use a strawberry basket.

Cc is for crystals.

Carlita went out shopping
With baby brother, Tom,
Looking for a birthday gift—
A big surprise for Mom.

They found a crystal necklace,
So shiny and so bright.
They knew that Mom would love it.
It was a pretty sight!

But when they saw the price tag,
They knew what they must do.
They started making crystals,
And now they have a slew!

JEWELRY

CRYSTAL CREATIONS

- pencil
- index card
- black construction paper
- blunt-tipped scissors
- glue

- 1/4 cup hot tap water
- disposable clear plastic cup
- 3 tablespoons Epsom salts
- measuring cup and spoons
- cotton swab
- yarn or string

1. Add Epsom salts to water. Mix well to dissolve.

2. Draw a shape on index card. Cut out. Trace onto black paper. Cut out.

3. Glue black paper shape onto index card shape.

4. Paint black side of shape with Epsom salts mixture. Let dry.

5. Punch hole in shape with pencil and add yarn to make a crystal pendant!

Dd is for drop.

Delilah is quite happy—
She loves a rainy day.
She grabs her boots and raincoat
And runs right out to play.

The rain is not a problem
Because her coat's so slick.
She never comes home soaking—
The water drops don't stick.

Drops slide right off her raincoat,
As if they're in a race.
That's why it is a raincoat—
Drops leave without a trace!

DROP DRAGSTER

What You'll Need:
- piece of cardboard
- sheet of white paper
- wax paper
- water
- watch with a second hand
- tape

1. Trace this racetrack onto white paper. Tape paper to cardboard.

2. Place wax paper over racetrack and tape it down.

wax paper
white paper
cardboard

3. Use finger to add drop. Tilt board to make drop go around track.

See how fast you can go!

FINISH

START

Don't let your drop touch the sides of the track!

 **is for egg.**

Ernesto is an egg cook.
He cooks them everyday.
He scrambles some and boils some,
Then puts the rest away.

He stores the eggs together,
The boiled ones with the raw.
Mixing up his egg supply—
A breaking of EGG LAW.

With all the eggs together,
Ernesto now must guess
Which eggs are the boiled ones,
Or risk a scrambled mess!

EGG-STRA EGG-CITEMENT

What You'll Need:
- hard-boiled egg
- raw egg
- 2 cereal bowls

1. Have partner place an egg in each bowl. Don't watch!

2. Spin each egg. Which one do you think spins faster?

3. Stop the spin with your finger, then quickly take your finger off. What happens?

4. Do you think you know which egg is which? Crack one open and see!

Ff is for float.

Frita floats upon the pond,
A happy little duck.
She never dives down under,
Into the bottom muck.

Her friends all throw her peanuts.
She eats them in a wink.
She has to catch them quickly,
Or else the peanuts sink.

Frita has some good advice
That slower ducks should note.
Moving to saltwater helps,
'Cause there the peanuts float!

FLOATING FEASTS

What You'll Need:

- 2 clear plastic disposable cups
- water
- 6 teaspoons of salt
- peanuts

- masking tape
- pencil

1. Use masking tape to label cups "fresh water" and "salt water".

2. Fill each cup almost full with water. Add salt to salt water cup and mix.

3. Pull the two halves of a peanut apart. Add one half to the fresh water. Add the other half to the salt water.

4. What happens to the peanut in each cup?

Gg is for glue.

Garretta loves her granny,
Who now has moved away.
Garretta used to see her
At least three times a day.

She wants to send a greeting
And has no time to waste.
Garretta finds her scissors,
Some paper and some paste.

She wants the card sent quickly—
But runs right out of glue.
Can she find some sticky stuff?
What will Garretta do?

MOO TO GLUE

What You'll Need:

- 2 tablespoons vinegar
- 1/2 cup warm milk
- 1/4 teaspoon baking soda
- measuring cup and spoons
- plastic straw for stirring
- 3 8-oz. paper cups
- small pieces of paper
- coffee filters

1. Stir warm milk into vinegar. Let mixture sit until solids form (about 3 minutes).

2. Pour mixture through coffee filter in the second cup. Let as much of the water drain as possible.

3. Scrape solids into third cup and stir in baking soda to make glue!

4. Test your glue by sticking a few small pieces of paper together and let dry overnight.

glue

5. Try to pull the paper pieces apart. How sticky was your glue?

 **is for helicopter.**

Meet Heather Helicopter,
A very funny name.
But that's what we call Heather—
Of helicopter fame.

Heather watches choppers fly—
Their blades spin 'round and 'round.
She likes to see them take off,
Then land back on the ground.

She wants to be a pilot,
Away up in the sky.
But 'til she gets her license,
She'll make toy choppers fly!

HAPPY HELICOPTERS

What You'll Need:
- 1 sheet of paper
- metric ruler
- blunt-tipped scissors
- paper clip

1. Trace helicopter pattern onto your own paper and carefully cut out.

2. Fold wing **A** toward you and wing **B** away. Add paper clip.

3. Hold your helicopter up high and drop. What happened?

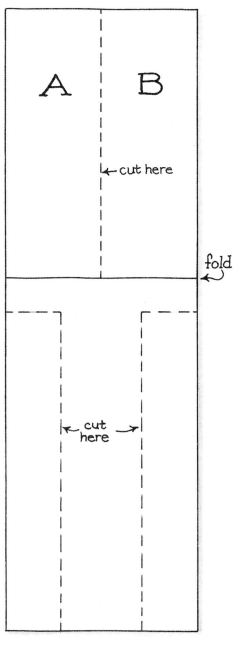

A   B

← cut here

fold ←

← cut here →

I i is for ice.

Ivy lives on Iceland Street.
Her house is made of ice.
She keeps her igloo chilly—
To her it feels so nice.

Then one day a heat wave hits,
And Ivy starts to sweat.
Her house is melting quickly,
Which causes her to fret.

What is Ivy going to do?
She wants to keep things cool,
So her igloo won't end up
Like water in a pool.

ICE ANTICS!

What You'll Need:

- 3 ice cubes
- aluminum foil
- white paper
- piece of fabric
- rubber bands
- 3 small paper plates

NOTE: Make sure your 3 ice cubes are all the same size.

1. Wrap up one ice cube in a small piece of aluminum foil. Place it on a plate.

2. Using rubber bands, wrap up the second ice cube in a small piece of paper. Place this cube on the second plate.

3. Wrap the third ice cube up in fabric. Use rubber bands to hold the fabric in place. Place this ice cube on the third plate.

4. Wait one hour.

5. Look at all these plates. Which one has the biggest puddle of water on it?

6. Now unwrap your ice cubes. What happened to your ice cubes? Which one melted the most? The least?

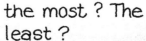

J j is for juice.

Jasper drives a juicemobile
Throughout the neighborhood.
He sells all kinds of juices
That look and taste so good.

He's made a juice from cabbage—
The flavor is brand new.
But customers won't drink it.
They don't like juice that's blue.

There is an easy answer—
Something that you can add
To change the juice's color,
And start a cabbage fad!

NEW JUICE USE

What You'll Need:

- red cabbage leaf
- warm water (about 1/2 cup)
- plastic zip-closing bag
- plastic cup
- vinegar
- teaspoon

1. Tear the cabbage leaf into small pieces and place in the plastic bag.

2. Add the warm water and close the bag tightly.

3. With your fingers, squish the cabbage leaves until the water turns blue. This is your cabbage juice.

Pour the cabbage juice back into the cup. Add a teaspoon of vinegar and mix well.

What happens to your cabbage juice?

K k

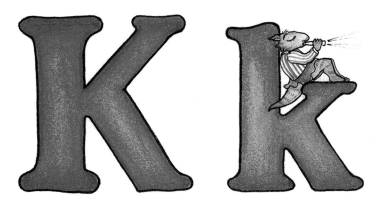

is for kazoo.

Konrad plays a mean kazoo
In Kay's Kazoo Quartet.
He's hardly ever nervous,
But now he's quite upset.

Konrad lost his best kazoo—
The big show starts at eight.
He needs to find another
Because the show won't wait.

Konrad doesn't worry much.
He knows what he can do.
He'll save the quartet's concert—
He'll make his own kazoo!

KAY'S
KAZOO
QUARTET

A KOOKY KAZOO!

What You'll Need:
- toilet paper tube
- wax paper
- rubber band

1. Cover one end with wax paper and a rubber band.

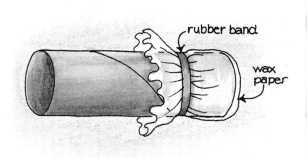

2. Hum into the open end. Try some different sounds.

3. Now hum without your kazoo. How is the sound different?

4. Experiment humming tunes and making different sounds with your own kazoo!

 **is for lens.**

Lenny likes to look at bugs
And other things so small—
Like ants and creepy crawlies,
Upon the garden wall.

Lenny looks for centipedes
And wiggly worms in dirt.
But 'cause he's always looking,
His eyeballs always hurt.

What helps him find these creatures,
In summer and in fall?
With a lens to magnify,
His eyes don't hurt at all!

LIQUID LENS

What You'll Need:

- large Styrofoam cup
- plastic wrap
- tape
- water

WARNING: Be careful of the cutting edge on the plastic wrap box. It's sharp!

1. Remove the rim of the styrofoam cup.

2. Cover one side with plastic wrap and tape down.

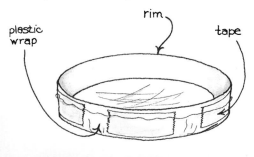

plastic wrap   rim   tape

3. Place 2-3 drops of water together inside to make a lens.

water drop

4. Look at these words through your water drop lens. What happens to the letters?

5. Look at a color picture in the newspaper or the stitches in stockings.

Comics

Mm is for magnet.

Makisha plays with magnets
At every chance she gets.
She uses them to make things,
For people and their pets.

One day while watching skaters
Slide by along the pond,
She thought of an invention—
A magnet wonder wand!

With paper clips and paper
Of course a magnet too
Try what young Makisha did—
It's so much fun to do!

MAGNETS ON THE MOVE

What You'll Need:

- white paper
- scissors
- tape
- paper clips
- construction paper
- markers or crayons
- ruler
- magnet

NOTE: Use a traditional round, square or rectangular magnet. Do not use flat sheet-type magnet.

1. Trace the skater below onto the paper and cut out. Bend the feet and tape them to two paper clips as shown.

TRACE→

← fold here

2. Tape two sheets of construction paper together for the base. With markers or crayons, draw a pond. Add some houses, trees or bridges.

Houses, trees and bridges are folded under bottom and taped on.

3. Tape the magnet onto the end of the ruler.

4. Place your skater on the pond and use your magnet wonder wand underneath to do some skating!

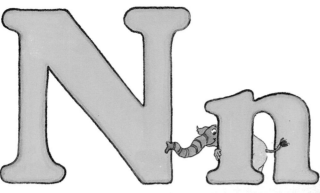

Nn is for nose.

Norbert sleeps the whole day through
And looks for food at night.
His special nose is handy,
Because there is no light.

So Norbert can sniff turnips,
Which grow below the ground,
He has a great schnozzola—
The longest one around.

His nose is so amazing,
That he can always tell
Where he can find the turnips,
From just their turnip smell!

NOSING AROUND

What You'll Need:

- blindfold
- pencil and paper
- orange piece
- celery piece
- peppermint stick
- piece of chocolate bar
- potato chip

1. Put on the blindfold. Make sure you can't see.

2. Have your partner place each of the food pieces on the table.

3. Smell each one. Try to guess what you are smelling.

Your partner can write down your guesses.

4. Now taste the pieces of food— one at a time. Try to guess what you are tasting.

5. Take off the blindfold. Were your guesses right?

O o is for ocean.

Ollie is a handyman,
The greatest one around.
He makes toys from odds and ends
And sells them by the pound!

While walking by the ocean,
And looking at the waves,
Ollie had a great idea—
A toy that would get raves!

So Ollie mixed up liquids
And added color, too.
See if you can do the same,
And make a toy for you!

OLLIE'S
POUND O' TOYS

OLLIE
POUND

OCEAN IN A BOTTLE

What You'll Need:

- large clear plastic soda bottle
- water
- blue food coloring
- light-colored cooking oil

1. Fill the bottle halfway with water.

2. Add a few drops of blue food coloring and mix.

3. Add oil until the bottle is filled to the very top. Cap tightly.

4. Turn the bottle sideways and tilt up and down. What do you see?

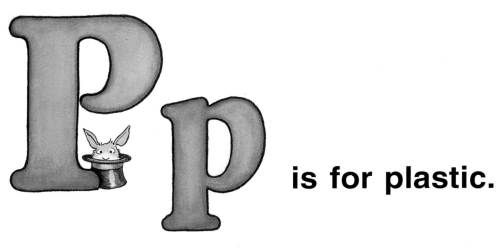

Pp is for plastic.

When Pam the great magician
Was eating lunch one day,
Some magic fans came over
And would not go away.

The people wanted magic,
But what was Pam to do?
She had her plastic lunch bag
And knew some science, too.

With a pencil from her purse
And her bag of plastic,
Take a look at what Pam did —
Totally fantastic!

FANTASTIC PLASTIC

What You'll Need:

- 1 zip-closing plastic bag
- pencil
- water
- paper towels

1. Fill the bag almost full with water and close tightly.

2. Hold the bag over the sink.

3. Slowly push the point of the pencil through one side of the bag.

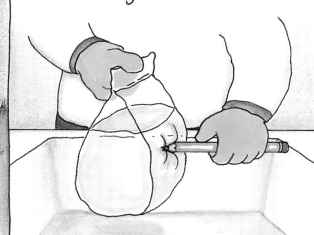

4. Now push the pencil all the way through the other side of the bag.

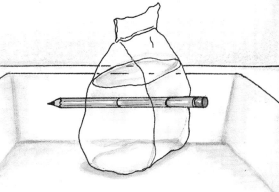

Did any water spill?

Qq is for quick.

Quincy and Quinona Quack
Are very quick indeed.
Everything they do is fast.
They move with lightning speed.

The quickness of those Quack kids
Is surely no mistake.
It took them years of practice,
'Cause quickness you can't fake.

Now Quincy and Quinona
Can teach you quickness, too.
So practice with the Quack kids
And learn what's quick for you!

QUICK QUACKERS

What You'll Need:

- cardboard
- blunt tip scissors
- pencil
- ruler
- black marker
- crayons

1. Cut a strip 2 inches wide by 20 inches long from the cardboard. Divide the strip into 5 equal parts.

2. Using the marker, label each band as shown and then color the bands.

20"

| LIGHTNING QUICK | QUICKER THAN QUICK | QUICK | LESS THAN QUICK | SNAIL-LIKE QUICK |

2"

4"

3. Have your partner hold the strip so that the red end is between your thumb and finger.*

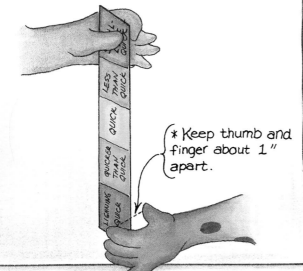

* Keep thumb and finger about 1" apart.

4. When your partner lets go of the strip, try to catch it. Which color did you grab? How quick are you?

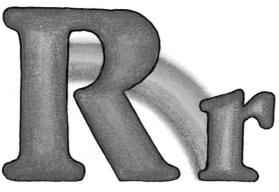

is for rainbow.

Rosie's always coloring—
It's what she likes to do.
She colors in the classroom.
She colors at the zoo.

One day when it stopped raining,
A rainbow soon appeared.
Young Rosie tried to paint it,
Before the rainbow cleared.

Rainbows never stay too long—
Their colors fade away.
Rosie needs some help from you
To make the colors stay!

RAINING RAINBOWS

What You'll Need:

- white unlined paper
- tape
- clear plastic audiocassette case
- flashlight

1. Tape the paper to the wall.

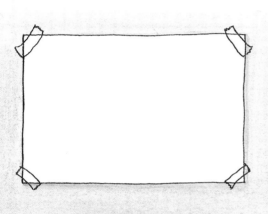

2. Turn on the flashlight and darken the room.

3. Shine the light through the case so that it hits the paper on the wall.

4. Tilt the case in different directions. Can you see the colors of the rainbow?

S s is for shadow.

Shirley gives a puppet show
For kids at all the schools.
At Halloween her puppets
Are goblins, ghosts, and ghouls.

The puppets Shirley uses
Aren't in the show at all.
Instead you see their shadows,
Way high upon the wall.

One of Shirley's puppets is
A creature, small and lean.
See what Shirley does with him
To make him big and mean!

SHIFTY SHADOWS

What You'll Need:

- pencil
- 1 unsharpened pencil
- blunt-tipped scissors
- paper

- tape
- flashlight
- dark room

1. Draw a small ghost and cut it out.

2. Tape your ghost to the end of a pencil.

3. In a dark room, use your flashlight to make a ghost shadow on the wall.

4. Move the flashlight or the ghost back and forth and see what happens on the wall.

T t 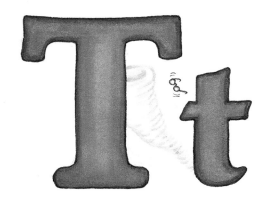 is for tornado.

Toto's daily science class
Has lots of things to do—
Activities with test tubes,
Experiments with goo.

Toto also reads about
The sun and clouds and rain.
He knows about tornadoes
That spin your weather vane.

Twisters twirl and spin and turn.
They lift things off the ground.
Now make your own tornado—
You won't get tossed around!

TWIST AND SPOUT

What You'll Need:

- 2 clear plastic soda bottles that are the same size
- tape
- water

1. Fill one of the bottles two-thirds full with water.

2. Tape the two bottles together tightly. Check for leaks.

tape

3. Turn the bottles over and swirl the top bottle.

4. What do you see in the bottle?

Uu  is for upside-down.

Umberto likes to see things
When he is upside-down.
What a different view he gets
From others in his town!

Umberto's getting tired
From standing on his head.
It's messing up his hairdo.
What could he do instead?

We need to help Umberto
Stand straight up on the street,
So things will look flipped over
When he stands on his feet!

UPSIDE-DOWN TOWN

What You'll Need:

- white paper
- magnifying glass

1. Choose a room with a big window to do this activity. Turn out the lights.

2. Stand with your back to the window. Hold the sheet of paper in one hand and the magnifying glass in the other hand.

3. Holding the paper still, move the magnifying glass back and forth until an image appears on the paper. What do you see?

IMPORTANT— To see the image, look directly at the paper, not through the magnifying glass.

 Don't let the sun shine directly through your magnifying glass!

V v

is for vegetable.

Vilma's always gardening
With shovel, spade, and hoe.
Celery's the vegetable
That Vilma loves to grow.

The stalks grow tall and sturdy
Into a leafy bunch.
It's a special vegetable,
'Cause it's got lots of crunch.

Sometimes when there is no rain,
The garden gets so dry.
Her celery starts drooping—
Help Vilma find out why!

VEGGIES WITH VIGOR!

What You'll Need:

- celery stalk
- disposable plastic cup
- water

- red food coloring
- butter knife

1. On a hot day, lay the celery stalk in the sun until it is very wilted.

2. Place a little water in the bottom of the cup. Add 10-15 drops of red food coloring and mix well.

3. Carefully cut off the base of the stalk. Place the stalk in the colored water.

4. Check the celery stalk every 30 minutes for the next four hours. What happens to your celery stalk?

 **is for wax.**

Wally had a secret thought
That he just had to tell.
Wendy sat four desks away—
He did not want to yell.

So Wally started thinking.
At first he had no clue
How he could send the message,
So Wendy would know, too.

How did our Wally do it
So no one else could see?
To send a secret message,
Some candle wax is key!

WAX 'N' WASH

What You'll Need:

- sheet of white paper
- white candle
- watercolor paint
- watercolor paintbrush
- water

1. Write a secret message with your candle.

WARNING: It will be very hard to see what you are drawing, but do the best you can.

2. Cover your message with watercolor paint.

3. Can you read the message?

Xx

is for xylophone.

Xena is a member of
A wild and crazy band.
They play all kinds of music—
They're really in demand.

Xanny's on the funnel horn,
While Xavier plays a pan.
Let's see what Xena's playing,
As loudly as she can.

Xena loves the xylophone,
And made her own one day
With some water and a spoon—
Hear how her bottles play!

HOME-GROWN XYLOPHONE !

What You'll Need:

- 6 identical glass soda bottles
- metal spoon
- ruler
- tape
- crayon
- sheet of paper
- water

1. Arrange your bottles in a row. Pour different amounts of water into each bottle so that the heights of the water are:

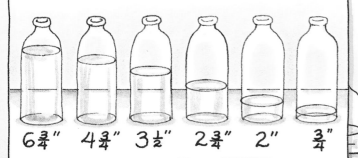

$6\frac{3}{4}"$ $4\frac{3}{4}"$ $3\frac{1}{2}"$ $2\frac{3}{4}"$ $2"$ $\frac{3}{4}"$

2. Gently tap on the side of each bottle with the spoon. Are the sounds you hear alike or different ?

3. Number the bottles from 1 to 6 as shown.

4. Play the tunes below or make up your own!

Mary Had a Little Lamb

```
3 2 1 2 3 3 3   2 2 2   3 5 5
3 2 1 2 3 3 3   3 2 2   3 2 1
```

Frère Jacques (Are You Sleeping?)

```
1 2 3 1   1 2 3 1   3 4 5   3 4 5
5 6 5 4 3 1   5 6 5 4 3 1
1 2 1   1 2 1
```

Yy is for you!

You're the only one like you—
You're special and unique!
Your walk, your talk, your laughter,
The way your eyeballs peek.

One look into your mirror
And you will surely see
Those parts that make you into
That person you call "me."

Those little things about you
That you have come to know
Make you that special someone—
You're YOU from head to toe!

YABBA-DABBA YOU!

What You'll Need:

- white unlined paper
- pencil
- clear tape

1. Trace your hand.

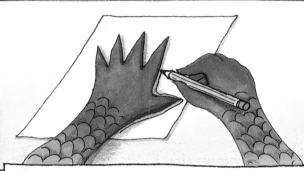

2. On another sheet of paper, use the pencil to rub an area as big as your finger. Make the area as black as possible.

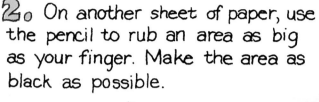

3. Rub your whole finger (not just the tip) back and forth in the black spot until you have a black smudge on your finger.

4. Press a piece of tape over the black smudge on your finger. The tape will pick up your finger print.

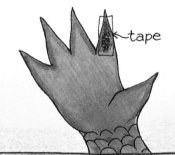
← tape

5. Stick the tape on your hand tracing.

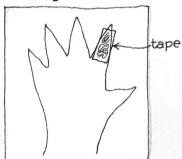
← tape

Repeat steps 2-5 for your other fingers and thumb.

6. Look at your finger prints. Which skin pattern do you have?

ARCH   LOOP   WHORL

 **is for zoom.**

Zach was walking home from school
And saw a sign that read:
"Come join a rocket contest,
And learn to zoom," it said.

Zach didn't have a rocket,
But knew that he could make
One that soared and zoomed real fast—
First prize he'd surely take.

With a bottle and a straw,
Zach zipped up to his room.
He built a flying rocket
That really had some zoom!

ZOOMERS!

What You'll Need:

- thin plastic coffee stirrer
- paper
- scissors
- tape
- straw
- empty dish detergent squeeze bottle (cap removed)

1. Cut out a half circle and tape it to make a cone. Leave a small opening at the tip.

tape 1"

2. Stick one end of the stirrer through the tip and tape it in place.

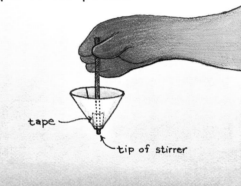

tape

tip of stirrer

3. Place the straw into the empty squeeze bottle and hold it in place with your hand. Try to seal the opening as much as possible.

4. Place your zoom rocket into the straw.

5. Give the bottle a hard squeeze.

Watch your rocket ZOOM!

WARNING: Be careful not to point your zoom rocket at anyone!

What's the Science Behind the Fun?

What makes Archie's apples turn brown?
Oxygen from the air mixes with certain substances in an apple, turning it brown when its protective skin is cut. The acid in lemon juice interferes with the reaction. Lemon juice often is sprinkled on cut-up apples and other fruit to keep them from turning brown.

Why does Benny use detergent to make his bubble liquid?
Bubble liquid in stores is made mostly of detergent and water. Tiny particles of detergent mix into and spread out over the water's surface, creating a thin film. The film stretches when air is blown into it, holding the air inside to make a bubble. What do you think happens when the film is stretched too thin?

How does Carlita make her crystals?
Crystals are substances made of tiny particles that fit together in a pattern that repeats itself. A crystal will have a certain number of flat sides, sharp edges, and pointy corners. Examples of crystals include sugar, snowflakes (ice crystals), diamonds, and salts, such as the Epsom salt in this activity. When the water used to dissolve the Epsom salt evaporates, the salt particles arrange themselves into a repeating pattern to form beautiful crystals.

Why don't water drops stick to Delilah's raincoat or racetrack?
The tiny particles that make up water are strongly attracted to each other. They stick together to form drops, but the plastic in a raincoat and the wax in the wax-paper racetrack are made from substances with oil in them. Water and oil are not attracted to each other, so the drops roll right off.

What keeps Ernesto's raw egg spinning after he lifts his finger?
The raw egg keeps spinning because its contents are liquid. Try swirling a glass of water and then setting the glass on a table. The water will keep on swirling for awhile. It's the same way with the liquid inside the egg. It keeps swirling after the egg is stopped and makes the whole egg spin again when it's released.

Why do Frita's peanuts float in salt water but not in fresh water?
Objects float if they're lighter than the amount of liquid that they displace, or push aside. They sink if they're heavier. Frita's peanuts are heavier than the fresh water that they displace, so they sink. Dissolving salt in fresh water makes the same amount of liquid heavier allowing Frita's peanuts to float. It's the same reason that you float more easily in the ocean than in a lake.

Why does Garretta use milk to make glue?
Milk has a protein in it called casein (KAY-seen). When vinegar is added to the milk, thick white lumps form that are mostly casein. The casein is attracted to the fibers in the paper, causing them to stick together. This bond strengthens as the glue hardens.

How does Heather's helicopter fly?
As the helicopter drops through the air, the air pushes against and around the paper propeller blades. That makes the helicopter spin. Placing a paper clip on the helicopter adds weight to make its flight more stable. Try flying your paper helicopter without a paper clip, and see what happens.

Why does one of Isabel's ice cubes melt faster than the others?
The ice cube wrapped in aluminum foil will melt before the one wrapped in paper and cloth. Because of its chemical make-up, aluminum transfers heat better than both paper and cloth, so heat from the room reaches the cube more quickly. Also, paper and cloth have air pockets among their fibers that trap heat and help keep it away from the cubes. The cubes stay frozen longer.

Why does Jasper's juice change colors?
The color of a substance depends partly on the chemicals in it. When vinegar is added to cabbage juice, a chemical reaction occurs, making a new chemical. This new chemical makes the juice a different color.

How does Konrad's kazoo make music?
When you hum into a kazoo, you cause the tube and the air inside to vibrate. These vibrations then cause the surrounding air to vibrate. When these vibrations reach the ears of listeners, they hear kazoo music.

Why does Lenny use a water drop to see better?
We see things because of the light rays that bounce off them. Light rays traveling through a water drop held at a certain distance bend to make the object look larger—the same way a magnifying glass works.

How does Makisha's magnet make her skaters move?
Metal paper clips contain iron, a metal that magnets attract. Magnets can work through many materials, including paper. The wonder wand magnet attracts the paper clips through the paper, allowing the skaters to skate.

How can Norbert find food from just its smell?
Norbert can smell things he cannot see because very tiny particles from those things are being carried in the air. When Norbert inhales, some of these tiny particles are carried up into his nose. Special parts inside his nose detect those particles and send a signal to his brain which recognizes the signal and tells him what he is smelling. Norbert finds food by moving in the direction where the smell is stronger.

How does Ollie's ocean-in-a-bottle work?
Oil and water stay apart because the tiny particles in water are very attracted to each other but not attracted to the particles in oil. Because water is more dense than oil, when the bottle is rocked, the water runs to the bottom, pushing the oil out of its way and making waves. (*Hint:* Adding color to the water makes it easier to tell the difference between the two liquids.)

Why does Pamela's plastic bag not spring a leak?

Plastic sandwich bags are flexible and stretching. When a sharp object, like a pencil point, is poked through the bag, the plastic squeezes around the pencil, making a tight, leak-proof seal. It's similar to the way that some tires on cars work. A gummy layer on the inside of the tire seals around any nails or sharp objects poking into the tire.

How can Quincy and Quinona (and you) get quicker?

Trying to catch the strip as soon as it is dropped is a way of testing reaction time. As soon as the strip is dropped, your eyes send a message to your brain that the strip is falling. Your brain then sends a message to your hand to close your fingers and catch it. With practice, your eyes, brain, and hand get used to working together and usually get quicker.

How does Rosie make her own rainbow?

Light from a flashlight, the sun, a candle, or other light source is made up of different colors or wavelengths of light. When light passes through certain objects—such as prisms, rain droplets, or a plastic cassette case—the different wavelengths can be bent at different angles. This makes the colors separate, so we see them as the individual colors of the rainbow.

How does Shirley make her shadows look so big?

The size of a shadow depends on three things: the size of the object, how far the object is from the light, and how far the object is from the surface where the shadow appears. With the object close to the flashlight, the farther Shirley holds her object (and flashlight) from the wall, the larger the shadow cast.

Why does Toto's swirling water look like a tornado?

Under certain conditions, liquid like water and the gases in air can act in similar ways. Wind swirling in a tornado and water swirling down a drain both create a shape called a *vortex*.

Why do Umberto's objects look upside-down?
When light rays pass through a magnifying lens, the rays are bent so that the top of the object appears at the bottom and the bottom of the object appears at the top. When the lens is held at a certain distance from the object and a piece of paper, the result is an upside-down image of the paper.

How does Vilma revive her wilted vegetables?
Celery, like all plants and other living things, is made up of cells. When its cells lose water through evaporation, celery wilts. But, when wilted celery is placed in water, the water moves up a long series of tube-like cells inside the stalk. Then the water moves into the rest of the cells. Once these cells are filled with water, the celery will stand straight.

Why does Wally choose wax to write his secret message?
All waxes contain fats or oils. Some wax is made from petroleum, which is a thick, dark oil from deep in the earth. Other waxes are made from animal fats or plant oils. Watercolor paint has water in it, and things that have water in them are not attracted to things that have oil in them. But, the paint *does* stick to the paper because it *is* attracted to the paper fibers.

How do Xena's bottles make different musical notes like a xylophone?
We hear sounds because of vibrations in the air. Longer objects vibrate more slowly and make lower-pitched sounds. Shorter objects vibrate faster and make higher-pitched sounds. When Xena strikes the bottles with a metal spoon, she causes the bottles and the water inside them to vibrate. The bottle with the most water makes the lowest-pitched sound. The bottle with the least water makes the highest-pitched sound.

What makes You different from everyone else?
The many things about you that make you different from everyone else are called *traits*. These traits come from special chemicals that make up your genes. You get your genes from your mother and father. Genes are kind of a recipe for you, with instructions for making your own special finger prints, freckles, straight or curly hair, and many other things about you.

What makes Zack's rocket zoom?

When anything flies, air pressure is always involved. Birds, airplanes, helicopters, footballs, and rockets all use air pressure and fight against it when they fly. For Zack's zoom rocket, a hard squeeze of the bottle creates high air pressure in the bottle. This high-pressure air rushes out of the bottle through the straw and pushes the rocket out of the bottle for its flight.

About the Book

The Authors

James Kessler currently is manager of the K−8 Science Office in the Education Division of the American Chemical Society (ACS). He has been the editor of ACS's *WonderScience* magazine, an elementary school hands-on science activity magazine since 1989. James also oversees the production and dissemination of other science educational materials for students and teachers in grades K−8 and conducts hands-on science workshops for pre- and in-service teachers. James received a B.A. in philosophy from Columbia University, a J.D. from Boston University School of Law, and a B.S. in science education from the University of Maryland. James has taught biology and physical science in the Washington, D.C. area and in Sao Paulo, Brazil.

Andrea Bennett, an experienced science teacher, now develops science teaching resources and administers a community science mini-grant program for ACS's K−8 Science Office. She also served as coordinating editor of the *ACS/USA Today* Explorations biweekly science column for children. Andrea currently conducts hands-on science workshops for children with the Smithsonian's Young Associates program. She holds bachelors degrees in both biology and science education from the University of Maryland.

The Illustrator

Melody Sarecky, a Corcoran School of Art graduate, has been illustrating for children's publications for 15 years, including *WORLD* Magazine, *HSUS News*, *Ranger Rick*, *Science Scope*, and *Weekly Reader*. Books that she has illustrated include *Serious Fun*, *Dragon's Lunch*, and *One Dad, Two Dads, Brown Dad, Blue Dads*.

The American Chemical Society

The **American Chemical Society (ACS)**, a non-profit professional organization of chemists, chemical engineers, and teachers, publishes the world's most prominent chemistry journals and serves as the leading information resource on chemical science and technology. The Society also develops science curricula, supports teacher training workshops, and provides science information for students of all ages and levels.

The **ACS Education Division** supports the development and implementation of programs that bring the wonder, excitement, opportunities, and challenges of modern chemistry to students of all ages. For more information about Education Division programs write to: Education Division, American Chemical Society, 1155 16th Street, N.W., Washington, DC 20036 or call (202) 452-2113.